ST. LOUIS, MISSOURI

A PHOTOGRAPHIC PORTRAIT

PHOTOGRAPHY BY BILL GRANT

First published in the United States of America by:

Twin Lights Publishers, Inc.
8 Hale Street
Rockport, Massachusetts 01966
Telephone: (978) 546-7398
http://www.twinlightspub.com

ISBN: 1-885435-77-0
ISBN: 978-1-885435-77-4

10 9 8 7 6 5 4 3 2 1

Photo on page 84 of the Mexican Gray Wolf is
courtesy of John Storjohann of the Wild Canid
Survival and Research Center.

Editorial researched and written by:
Francesca and Duncan Yates
www.freelancewriters.com

Book design by:
SYP Design & Production, Inc.
www.sypdesign.com

Printed in China.

GATEWAY TO THE WEST

In 1765, eleven years before the birth of America, a group of French fur traders from New Orleans traveled 1278 miles up the Mississippi River to a scenic spot just eighteen miles from the confluence of the Mississippi and Missouri Rivers. Strategically, it was a perfect place to establish a trading post for doing business with Native American tribes in the vast lands to the west.

St. Louis evolved around this trading post, thriving on its central location and natural river highways. It soon became an important player in contributing to the growth of a young nation.

In 1803, Napoleon Bonaparte, Emperor of France, made a secret real estate deal with President Thomas Jefferson that doubled the size of America overnight. The historically documented Louisiana Purchase states that Bonaparte sold to America 800,000 square miles of French-owned lands between the Mississippi River and the Rocky Mountains, setting the stage for America's phenomenal growth and development.

From that moment on, St. Louis' future was in fast-forward mode. Meriwether Lewis and William Clark set out from St. Louis a year later on their historic expedition to chart the new territory and find a direct water route to the Pacific.

St. Louis quickly became a major outfitting port for mountain men, adventurers and pioneers bound for glory and prosperity in the western frontier. Vast fortunes were made by the town's merchant-entrepreneurs. Mississippi riverboats lined up for miles, waiting to transport people and supplies. By the end of the 19th century, the era of westward exploration would close triumphantly, and St. Louis would remain firmly set on the world map.

Today nearly three million people live in the Greater St. Louis area, infusing it with a distinct charm and personality along with a passionate pride in its heritage. This prosperous Midwestern city has flourished with industry, commerce, and an impressive collection of nationally-ranked, research universities, world-class museums, cultural venues, city parks and historic neighborhoods. And when the sun goes down, St. Louis' nightlife never disappoints. The city's musical heritage dates back to the ragtime beat of Scott Joplin, who changed the way an entire generation tapped their feet.

This photographic keepsake celebrates a kaleidoscope of memorable images by photographer, Bill Grant, that resonate with the true spirit of St. Louis.

Kiener Plaza

Nestled in downtown St. Louis, against the backdrop of the Old Courthouse and the magnificent Gateway Arch, Kiener Plaza is the city's heartbeat, a place for joyous city festivals, raucous sports rallies and victory celebrations.

Forest Park *(above and opposite)*

Five hundred acres larger than New York's Central Park, this St. Louis treasure is one of 105 city parks that frame this riverside city and provide a refreshing oasis of outdoor recreational activities. The abundant attractions of Forest Park draw over twelve million visitors yearly, many of whom enjoy paddling canoes on the park's tree-shaded waterways and stopping for a picnic or lunching at a dockside restaurant.

Beauty of St. Louis

Forest Park's sprawling acres of green space
are beautifully landscaped and dotted with
monuments, historic buildings, wildlife and
waterways. The park is also home to the St.
Louis Zoo, the Muny Opera House and major
museums.

Carondelet Park

One of the city's oldest parks, Carondelet attracts St. Louisans with its scenic lakes, rolling hills, picnic areas, playgrounds, tennis courts and ballparks. The park's 19th-century Lyle House is an evocative link to the early history of the area.

Gateway Mall

Running from the magnificent Gateway Arch
on the east to Union Station on the west, the
Gateway Mall adds refreshing, green space to
the downtown area. It is a favorite gathering
place for parades, concerts, festivals and other
events.

"The Meeting of The Waters"

Aloe Plaza's showpiece is a massive fountain and bronze sculpture by Swedish artist Carl Milles. Two nudes symbolize the convergence of the Mississippi and Missouri Rivers. Water spirits represent seventeen smaller streams.

Tower Grove Park *(top and bottom)*

Tower Grove Park is a faithful reflection of the refined taste and sensibilities of its benefactor, St. Louis merchant Henry Shaw. To the delight of visitors, this 19th-century park has playful Victorian pavilions and sculptures that were commissioned by Shaw. He personally supervised the landscaping by importing thousands of trees and shrubs from around the world. Here, the summer air is always filled with the aroma of seasonal blossoms, the sounds of children at play and the music of live concerts.

Now and Forever

Reminiscent of Roman ruins, this quaint corner of Tower Grove Park provides an idyllic setting for a wedding to remember. Benefactor Henry Shaw believed that parks must be *"conducive to the health and happiness of its inhabitants."*

13

"The Way" 1972–1980 by Alexander Liberman

Formerly the 72-acre estate of St. Louis philanthropist Mrs. Henry Laumeier, the Laumeier
Sculpture Park has developed into an internationally recognized open-air museum. The park col-
lects and exhibits monumental contemporary art.

Tower Grove House and Kaeser Maze

The creation of the botanical gardens was the lifelong passion of St. Louis philanthropist and humanitarian Henry Shaw. His country estate, Tower Grove House, was landscaped with the formal English labyrinth design.

Tropical Plants and Glass Onions

The Gardens' geodesic domed conservatory houses over a thousand tropical plant species amidst waterfalls and pools. Famed glass sculptor Dale Chihuly's *Walla Walla Onions, 2006* decorates a reflecting pool outside.

Chihuly at the Gardens

Ranked in the top three worldwide, the Missouri Botanical Gardens are the oldest in the United States, constantly delighting visitors with stunning gardens and collections, exceptional architecture and inspirational fountains and statuary. The blue shapes rising out of the fountain is *Polyvitro Crystal Tower, 2006,* by internationally acclaimed artist Dale Chihuly. His glass sculptures are part of a temporary exhibit, "Glass in the Garden: Chihuly at the Missouri Botanical Gardens."

Doris I. Schnuck Children's Garden

This special place at the botanical gardens is a *Missouri Adventure* that brings botany and 19th-century history to life with interactive themes. Visit a Midwestern prairie village, explore a limestone cave, scream down the Spelunker's Slide, discover the wetlands and board a Mississippi riverboat. The Children's Garden is challenging and fun for all.

St. Louis Riverfront Trail *(top)*

Connecting the eleven-mile stretch along the
Mississippi River between the Gateway Arch
and Riverfront Park, this greenway follows the
St. Louis Floodwall, various levees, historic
neighborhoods and showcases wildlife and
native plants.

One River Mississippi *(bottom)*

Designed to celebrate the ecosystem of the
Mississippi River, this unique performance
arts project features seven simultaneous performances in riverfront cities from the river's
headwaters to the Gulf of Mexico.

Basilica of St. Louis, King of France *(opposite)*

The oldest cathedral west of the Mississippi, it held the first mass in St. Louis in 1764. Pope John XXIII personally elevated it to a "basilica" in 1961. Today, it is a treasured landmark and the only building on the Gateway Arch grounds.

St. Louis Skyline *(above)*

Soaring much higher than the tallest skyscrapers, the elegant sweep of Gateway Arch frames a riverside view of St. Louis. With its massive size, the Arch pays fitting tribute to St. Louis' pivotal role in westward expansion.

Kiener Plaza Waterfall *(above)*

Cascading down the center of Kiener Plaza near "The Runner" statue, the waterfall flows from the Overlook Stage down to the May Amphitheater. Both stages are popular venues for live concerts and other public events.

"The Runner" *(opposite)*

Bathed in the warm glow of lampposts and floodlights, the Old Courthouse sets the mood for "The Runner," a bronze statue in Kiener Plaza commissioned by the park's namesake, steel executive and former Olympic high-hurdler, Henry Keiner.

A Matter of Taste

Union Station's special appeal is its delightful mix of ninety-plus specialty retail shops, offering everything from one-of-a-kind gifts, designer fashions, 20th-century train memorabilia, baseball fine art and the great taste of gourmet fudge.

Union Station

Modeled after a walled, medieval city in southern France, Union Station is a mixture of Romanesque styles with its 65-foot barrel-vaulted ceiling, stained glass windows, gold leaf detailing, and sweeping staircase in the Grand Hall.

Shopping at Union Station *(above)*

At one time the busiest and largest railroad terminal in the world, elegant Union Station became the largest adaptive re-use project in the United States, offering a dazzling variety of shopping, dining and entertainment.

Meet Me in St. Louis *(opposite)*

After a $150-million renovation in the 1980s, this national historic landmark began the second stage of its illustrious career as a shopping, dining and entertainment complex. It is also home to the luxurious Hyatt-Regency Hotel.

Atop St. Louis (above)

On the way to the thrilling view at the top of this majestic, 630-foot monument, tram riders enjoy history lessons with exhibits that transport them back to the 19th-century waterfront and the day in 1965 when the final Arch section was set in place.

Modern Masterpiece (opposite)

In the surreal night of a full moon, the Gateway Arch rises out of the ground like a giant elephant tusk. In reality, the Arch is a stainless-steel masterpiece of modern design by architect Eero Saarinen and is built to last one thousand years.

Gateway Arch (pages 30–31)

The signature structure that defines the skyline, the Gateway Arch celebrates the city's historic role as the gateway to the West. It is part of the Jefferson National Expansion Memorial honoring Thomas Jefferson's role in opening the West.

Westward Expansion Museum *(top)*

This unique museum, located at the Gateway Arch, exhibits rare artifacts from the days of Lewis and Clark. Visitors experience the opening of the West via interactive, life-like animatronic figures, movies, an authentic covered wagon, an actual teepee and Sioux war bonnet.

From Sea to Shining Sea *(bottom)*

Soon after America bought the Louisiana Territory from France in 1803, Thomas Jefferson hired Lewis and Clark to chart the new lands and find a direct water route to the Pacific. Their historic expedition embarked from St. Louis.

View from The Top

Rising 630 feet above St. Louis, the Gateway Arch offers an extraordinary view of the city and surrounding communities. On a clear day, tourists can see for miles in all directions and enjoy a bird's eye view of the Mighty Mississippi.

Historic First Missouri State Capitol *(above)*

Enter this ordinary 19th-century building and discover the restored, fully furnished rooms where Missouri's first legislators met to transform the territory of Missouri into a state. Also exhibited is the private residence and store of the building's original owners.

Old Courthouse Reflections *(opposite)*

Before the original 1828 courthouse was built, city business was conducted in various locations such as in a church, a tavern and a fort. Due to a booming fur trade, St. Louis grew rapidly, requiring a larger courthouse, which was further expanded to today's structure.

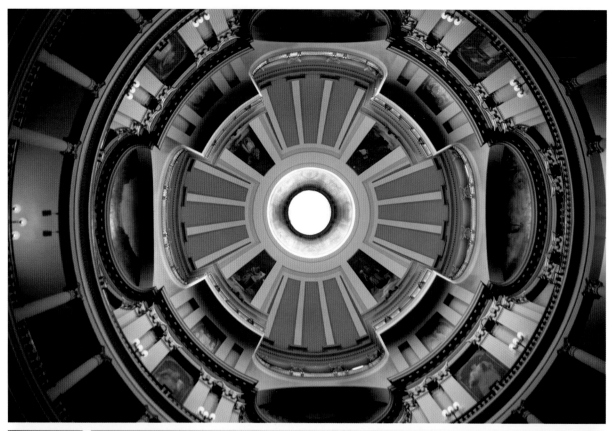

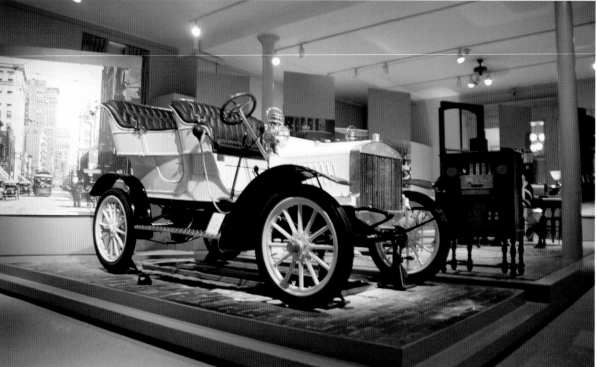

Old Courthouse Dome *(top)*

The richly detailed interior of the Old Courthouse's magnificent Italian Renaissance dome is distinguished by four historical lunette murals by noted St. Louis artist Carl Wimar.

Old Courthouse Museum *(bottom)*

The Old Courthouse is filled with the rich history of St. Louis' pivotal role in America's westward expansion. Visitors enjoy artifacts, exhibits, renovated 19th- and 20th-century courtrooms and unique dioramas of major historical events.

Historic Legal Trials

In the mid 1800s, St. Louis' Old Courthouse found itself embroiled in hundreds of suits for freedom filed by Missouri slaves. The most famous case involved Dred Scott and his wife, Harriet, who won their law suit and were granted their freedom in a decision that was subsequently overturned by the Supreme Court, leading to the outbreak of the Civil War. The courthouse is nationally recognized as part of the Freedom Network of the Underground Railroad.

Holocaust Museum and Learning Center

Located on the grounds of the Jewish
Community Center, this is a very personal
museum for St. Louis. It tells the story of the
Holocaust through the eyes of survivors, many
of whom lived in the Lodz Ghetto of Poland
and later moved to St. Louis.

America's Center and Edward Jones Dome

Offering much more than state-of-the-art meeting space, America's Center Convention Center has an intimate concert hall and an imaginative and versatile dome design that easily transforms exhibition space into a football field or concert venue.

Black Repertory Company *(top)*

As the nation's largest professional African-American theatre company, this distinguished organization produces exceptional professional dramas, comedies and musicals by primarily African-American and third-world play-wrights.

City Hall *(bottom)*

Built on Market Street in 1893, this elegant, granite and brick building was inspired by French architecture and the City Hall of Paris. Although the functions of many original rooms changed, the mayor's office has remained the same.

Powell Symphony Hall

After an extensive, two-million-dollar renovation, the historic St. Louis Theatre, an old vaudeville venue, was transformed into one of the finest concert halls in America and the first permanent home of the St. Louis Symphony.

41

Central West End *(top and bottom)*

Central West End, an historic area of stately 19th-century mansions north of Forest Park, is now a vibrant and cosmopolitan gathering place with trendy restaurants, bars, chic boutiques, art galleries, and antique shops.

Diners at a Central West End sidewalk café have more to look at than their menus in this bustling neighborhood where the action seldom slows down. Friendly bars and four-star restaurants keep the night lights on into the wee morning hours.

Historic Laclede's Landing *(opposite)*

Originally an 18th-century fur trading post, Laclede's Landing is the birthplace of St. Louis. Today, the surrounding nine-block area of cobblestone streets and historic buildings teems with outstanding shopping, dining and entertainment.

Casino Queen

Tourists and St. Louisans who are in the mood
for riverboat gambling, elaborate buffets and
star-studded entertainment can board this
floating casino, a replica of a 19th-century
side-wheeler riverboat, docked across the river
from the Gateway Arch.

Riverboat

A riverboat sightseeing cruise is the best way to experience Old Man River and the city of St. Louis from the waterline. Passengers learn about the important role St. Louis and other river cities played in America's great expansion westward.

St. Louis Icon

From any point in the city, the majestic curve
of the Gateway Arch can be seen towering
over the tallest skyscrapers, a constant
reminder of the city's unparalleled role in
promoting westward expansion.

Admiral Casino (top)

Even though this riverboat doesn't cruise, the *Admiral* offers its guests four decks of casino fun. Permanently docked at St. Louis' historic Laclede's Landing, a lively entertainment district, the *Admiral* is one of the riverboat casinos in St. Louis.

Tom Sawyer Riverboat (bottom)

No name conjures up bygone days on the mighty Mississippi like *Tom Sawyer*. This replica of the great 19th-century steamboats plies the waters day and night with sightseeing tours, romantic dinner cruises and private charters for weddings and holiday parties.

Cathedral Basilica of St. Louis

This majestic cathedral rises over St. Louis' chic Central West End with stunning architecture that blends 4th-century Byzantine style (large dome) with the 11th-century Romanesque style of arches and vaulted ceilings. The richly detailed interior of the basilica dome is resplendent with elaborate mosaics that were gradually added from 1914 to 1988. Today, the cathedral contains the world's most extensive collection of mosaic art.

Fox Theatre

After suffering the familiar decline of many of America's great movie palaces during the Great Depression, the opulent Fox Theatre came back to dazzling life in the 1980s, meticulously restored to its 1929 splendor. Originally dubbed "The Temple of the Motion Picture," the Fox now hosts the best of Broadway's road-show musicals, internationally renowned concert performances of music, ballet, modern dance, and solid-gold favorites from the 1960s.

Fourth of July Fireworks

Brilliant fireworks are only part of the nonstop
fun built into Fair St. Louis, a four-day joyous
celebration downtown with live concerts,
delectable foods, all culminating in the spec-
tacular 4th of July firework display.

Pagent Nightclub at The Loop *(top)*

Northwest of Forest Park, this trendy neighborhood attracts crowds with 120 unique stores and boutiques, 40 diverse dining spots, and the state-of-the-art Pageant nightclub, headlining hot rockers and rappers and premier comedy acts.

Pin-Up Bowl at The Loop *(bottom)*

This chic bowling alley with its signature martini lounge is one of only 30 bars, clubs and lounges around the globe to receive Conde Nast Traveler's "Hot Nights Award for 2004."

St. Louis University *(above)*

The oldest university west of the Mississippi River and the second oldest Jesuit university in the nation, St. Louis University, in the heart of downtown, attracts the nation's and world's brightest students.

St. Francis Xavier College Church *(opposite)*

Easily the university's most familiar landmark, the lofty steeple of this Irish Gothic church towers over the urban campus from a hill that rises gradually from the Mississippi. Completed in 1884, "College Church" as it is nicknamed, is the second church in St. Louis (the Old Cathedral was the first) to hold regular services. The exquisite stained glass windows of this white stone church are styled after Paris' famous Chartres Cathedral.

St. Louis University *(top and bottom)*

Ranked among the top research institutions in America, the Jesuit university also has a campus in Madrid, Spain, where it is the first U.S. institution recognized as an official foreign university by Spain's higher education authority. Every year 8,000 applicants compete for 1,500 freshmen slots at prestigious St. Louis University. The first school west of the Mississippi to grant a medical degree, its student population now exceeds 11,000 undergraduates and graduates.

Historic Samuel Cupples House *(opposite)*

The former home of a 19th-century multi-millionaire entrepreneur, this distinctive mansion on the university campus doubles as a fine arts gallery and a stately venue for university functions, weddings, and other special events.

New and Old Busch Stadiums (*top and bottom*)

It was out with the old and in with the new at the end of the 2005 season as the St. Louis Cardinals and nostalgic fans bid a formal farewell to the old Busch Stadium (*bottom*) that had seen forty, sell-out seasons of professional baseball since the 1960s. A brand-new, state-of-the-art stadium (*top*) was getting the finishing touches right next door, just in time for the 2006 season and a World Series victory. The old stadium was the last of the much-maligned cookie-cutter stadiums of the 1960s and '70s.

Busch Stadium

The new Busch Stadium is designed to deliver the best views in baseball. Concourses are open so fans won't miss the action while getting refreshments, and from nearly all of the 50,000 seats, fans enjoy fantastic views of the city skyline.

St. Louis Cardinals Hall of Fame

Across from Busch Stadium, inside the International Bowling Museum, the Cardinals Hall of Fame showcases over one-hundred years of St. Louis baseball. Fans enjoy soaking up the rich history of their favorite team through photographs and memorabilia from the 1880s to the present, including nine world championships, fifteen National League pennants, and World Series rings. Rare artifacts from the Negro National League are also displayed.

Race for The Home-Run Record *(top)*

Cardinal fans know exactly what this scoreboard means. It was the 1998 race between veteran first baseman Mark McGwire and outfielder Sammy Sosa for the major league single-season home-run record. McGwire won by four home runs.

Ozzie Smith *(bottom)*

Even though every generation has their own favorites, Ozzie Smith, the outstanding Cardinals shortstop known for his signature "backflips," is a favorite with all fans. He generously donated his personal memorabilia to the museum.

Beall Mansion Bed & Breakfast

Guests at the Beall Mansion B&B are quickly immersed in the opulent lifestyle of the privileged class at the turn of the 20th century, in a setting of crystal chandeliers, hardwood floors, leaded glass windows, fine art and sculpture and Persian rugs.

Million-Dollar Mansion

Now an elegant bed and breakfast on "Millionaire's Row" in nearby, historic Alton, Illinois, Beall Mansion was once the private residence of noted Senator Edmond Beall, politician, industrialist, and financier.

Eugene Field House *(left)*

Known as the "Children's Poet," published poet Eugene Field was the first to write a personal column in daily newspapers. His infamous father, attorney Roswell Martin Field, helped slave Dred Scott sue for his family's freedom in the Old Courthouse.

St. Louis Toy Museum *(right)*

Eugene Field's boyhood home is an appropriate home for the St. Louis Toy Museum. The vintage collection of 19th-century dolls and toys celebrates Field's lifelong passion for collecting these childhood treasures.

Childhood Treasures

This remarkable, permanent collection of nostalgic dolls and toys is showcased amidst many authentic furnishings of the Field family. The children's poet became famous for writing "Little Boy Blue" and "Wynken, Blynken, and Nod."

The King of Ragtime *(opposite)*

The future was bright for musical genius Scott Joplin when he moved into this house on Delmar Boulevard with his new bride, Belle, in 1902. *Maple Leaf Rag* was a tremendous success, soon to be followed by many more ragtime classics.

Scott Joplin House *(top)*

The Joplin home, which is a Missouri State Park, was a walk-up flat in St. Louis' blue-collar district, densely populated by African-Americans and German immigrants. Joplin worked his musical magic in the nearby honkytonks and bawdy houses of Chestnut Valley.

The Entertainer *(bottom)*

A national historic landmark, Scott Joplin's house is dedicated to his life and the flamboyant music that defined an important musical era. Joplin composed over 50 pieces, including *The Entertainer* and *Elite Syncopations*.

Cahokia Mounds State Historic Site

Eight miles east of downtown St. Louis is one
of the most exciting archeological finds in
North America. It is the great capital of a
pre-historic Native American culture called
the Mississippians who inhabited the land
one thousand years ago.

Cahokia Mounds Interpretive Center *(top)*

The 2200 acres of this historic site show all the signs that this was a significant cultural and spiritual center of the Mississippians. It is very possible that the ancient walled village of Cahokia was the Mecca or Vatican of its time.

Temple Mounds *(bottom)*

There are dozens of flat-topped mounds throughout the site. Some are temple mounds where the village leaders lived while others are burial mounds. A Woodhenge structure indicates a prehistory understanding of astronomy and seasons.

Faust Historic Village *(top)*

Nine 19th-century buildings were moved here to create this historic village, including an 1880 German-style carriage house, a log cabin with two rooms connected by a breezeway, barns, smokehouses and a blacksmith shop.

The Way It Was *(bottom)*

Weekend visitors enjoy guided tours by historical re-enactors in authentic, period costumes who discuss the village's ongoing restoration process, construction techniques and the lifestyle of the 19th-century families who lived there.

Faust County Park

Faust Historical Village is one of many attractions at Faust County Park which include the Sophia M. Sachs Butterfly House, St. Louis Carousel, St. Louis Symphony Music School and Thornhill, the estate of a former Missouri governor.

Columbia Bottom

The Missouri Conservation Department pur-
chased Columbia Bottom, a 4,318-acre area at
the confluence of the Missouri and Mississippi
Rivers to create a mosaic of protected bottomland habitats.

Wildlife Habitats

Columbia Bottom's new access roads and walkways bring visitors into the heart of pristine, shallow wetlands, bottomland hardwoods, prairie and crop lands to witness the resident and migratory wildlife these protected areas attract.

Prairie Grass in the Mist

At the confluence of Missouri's largest rivers,
this urban conservation area includes several
miles of river frontage, hundreds of acres of
bottomland forest, a 110-acre island and over
three-thousand acres of prairie cropland.

Where Eagles Soar

Birding is a rewarding and exciting hobby along the Mississippi and Missouri Rivers. In January and February, birders can watch majestic eagles soar in the wild from a large viewing platform at Columbia Bottom.

Lessons of Nature

From April to September, Columbia Bottom
sponsored special events to bring people of all
ages to this pristine, natural treasure, including bike rides, hikes, and career day with a
special appearance by Smokey the Bear.

The Power of the Mississippi

Shown on maps from the mid 1800s, a small town known as Columbia and later as St. Vrain, was located in this river bottom. By 1870, the river reclaimed the town which disappeared from future maps.

Owl Butterfly *(opposite)*

The Owl, Clipper, Paper Kite, Archduke, Red Lacewing, Common Blue Morpho, Orange Julia and the Postman—these are the resident species at the Conservatory. On any day, additional species may make a surprise appearance.

Butterfly House, Faust County Park *(above)*

Housed within the dramatic, glass-enclosed Conservatory is the beauty of thousands of exotic butterflies in flight amidst a lush flower garden. Outside, native butterflies soar free.

Sandy Creek Covered Bridge *(above)*

Back in 1872, six picturesque bridges were built to connect the Jefferson County seat of Hillsboro with St. Louis. Today the Sandy Creek Bridge is the only one remaining and one of just four covered bridges in the entire state of Missouri.

Shaw Nature Reserve *(opposite)*

The Reserve, which is an extension of the Missouri Botanical Garden, is crisscrossed with scenic hiking trails through wetlands, glades, upland and bottomland forests, wildflower gardens, native and exotic conifers, tall-grass prairies, and the Meramec River.

Mexican Gray Wolf

A half-hour from St. Louis, the world-famous, nonprofit Wild Canid Survival and Research Center, founded by noted naturalists Marlin and Carol Perkins, was the first place to successfully breed the Mexican gray wolf in captivity in 1981. Known also as the Wolf Sanctuary, it is home to Mexican red wolves and more Mexican gray wolves than any other captive breeding or zoological facility in the country. It is located on the Washington University campus in Eureka.

World Bird Sancuary

A unique St. Louis attraction, the sanctuary is devoted to securing the future of birds of prey in their natural habitats and is home to an impressive array of eagles, owls, hawks, falcons, vultures, parrots, mammals and reptiles.

World Bird Sanctuary *(above)*

Visitors can see many birds of prey at the World Bird Sanctuary, including peregrine falcons. Highly adaptive, these raptors live on every continent except Antarctica. They are known for their amazing, high-speed dives.

American Barn Owl *(opposite)*

The sanctuary has an impressive number of American Barn Owls and their European counterparts. These sixteen-inch owls nest in cavities or barns instead of building nests and fly silently as a result of sound-dampening fringes on their wings.

A Crown of Feathers *(left)*

East African crowned cranes are regal, intelligent birds who live in open wetlands and grasslands, dining on grass seeds, insects, frogs and lizards. To protect their young, parents will pretend to be injured to lure predators away from their young.

New Beginnings *(right)*

A gangly, baby giraffe stands tentatively while his mother protectively nurtures him. Awkward now, the baby will grow to sixteen feet tall, with keen eyesight and the natural ability to run as fast as a race horse.

St. Louis Zoo

Shortly after the 1904 Louisiana Purchase Exposition brought the world's attention to St. Louis, the idea for a zoo was born. Today, the highly acclaimed zoo is one of the best in the country, with 5000 animals from 700 species.

The Jewel Box *(top)*

An outstanding example of greenhouse
design, the Jewel Box in Forest Park opened
in 1936 to rave reviews across the country.
The St. Louis Post-Dispatch called the Art
Deco-style structure *"the latest word in display
greenhouses."*

Gathering Among the Flowers *(bottom)*

After extensive renovations, including a heat-
ing and air conditioning system along with a
catering area, this national historic site is now
an ideal setting for wedding receptions, corpo-
rate meetings and other gatherings.

The Jewel of Forest Park *(opposite)*

After a $3.5 million renovation, the Jewel Box
sparkles again. Its unconventional, can-
tilevered vertical glass walls rise five stories
above permanent floral displays, fountains,
reflecting pool and breathtaking, seasonal
flowers.

Firemen's Memorial *(left)*

Facing the entrance to City Hall, Firemen's Memorial was dedicated in 1994 to "St. Louis firefighters past, present and future." Artist R.P. Daus' bronze sculpture on a granite pedestal depicts a young child safe in the arms of a courageous firefighter.

Poet of Freedom *(right)*

"It is through beauty that one proceeds to freedom." These are the words of Friedrich Schiller, an influential 18th-century poet and playwright whose works on human rights and political freedom inspired opposition to tyranny worldwide.

Liberty is Not License *(opposite)*

Commissioned to commemorate the founding of the American Legion, this sculptured granite pylon by Sascha Schnittman was criticized as being too modern in conception in 1942. Atop the shaft is the eternal "Flame of Freedom."

IN COMMEMORATION OF
THE FOUNDING OF THE
AMERICAN LEGION IN
SAINT LOUIS MAY 1919
BORN OF SERVICE AND
COMRADESHIP IN THE
GREAT WAR OF 1917-18
DEVOTED TO GOD AND
COUNTRY

DEDICATED
SEPTEMBER 6, 1942

ON THIS SITE
WAS BORN
THE AMERICAN LEGION
MAY 8-9-10, 1919

LIBERTY IS
NOT LICENSE

THE AMERICAN LEGION
DEPARTMENT OF MISSOURI
COMMEMORATES THE
FIFTIETH ANNIVERSARY
OF THE FOUNDING OF
THE AMERICAN LEGION
IN SAINT LOUIS

MAY 10, 1969

World War II Memorial *(above)*

Titled *Court of Honor*, this 1948 monument to the victims of World War II is a striking forty-foot, limestone pillar in the shape of a broken sword with low-relief soldiers in battle on its base. It is a companion to the World War I memorial.

Historic Compton Hill Water Tower *(opposite)*

Once there were hundreds of water towers in America. Today, three of only seven that remain, are located in St. Louis. After extensive renovations to the richly detailed French Romanesque style structure, it is open for tours and panoramic views of the city.

Jefferson Barracks Historic Park *(opposite)*

A major Army post from 1826 to 1946, Jefferson Barracks played a vital role in westward expansion. It was a gathering and distribution point for troops and supplies headed to combat in all conflicts from the Mexican War through World War II.

Historic Stable *(above)*

Built in 1851, the stable housed four horses and two spring wagons that hauled munitions between the St. Louis Arsenal and the Barracks. Visitors today enjoy river views, museums, amphitheater, ball fields, and a paved hiking trail.

Soldier's Memorial Military Museum

Visitors to this downtown memorial museum
enjoy its impressive collection of historic military artifacts. Two spacious exhibit rooms are
filled with uniforms, medals, photographs,
weaponry, posters, war souvenirs and military
regalia.

Virtues of a Soldier's Life

The entrance to the Soldiers Memorial Museum is embellished with four stone sculptures that represent virtues in a soldier's life: Courage and Vision stand at the south stairs while Loyalty and Sacrifice stand at the north stairs.

Missouri History Museum

In 1866, the founding members organized the Missouri Historical Society "for the purpose of saving from oblivion the early history of the city and state." Today, the Society operates the acclaimed Missouri History Museum in the Beaux-Arts Jefferson Memorial Building, the first national monument to the nation's third president. Jefferson oversaw the Louisiana Purchase which signaled St. Louis' pivotal role in America's great westward expansion to the Pacific.

96

Thomas Jefferson *(left)*

At the entrance of the Missouri History Museum is a statue of Thomas Jefferson by noted sculptor Karl Bitter. Inside, the interactive "Seeking St. Louis" exhibition illustrates the history of the region from earliest times to the present and encompasses two exhibit halls.

Spirit of St. Louis *(right)*

Suspended high in the museum's rafters is a finely crafted replica of the *Spirit of St. Louis*, the plane Charles Lindbergh flew in his historic, non-stop flight from New York to Paris in 1927. With Boeing's plant nearby, aviation continues to be a significant industry.

Lewis and Clark Boat House and Nature Center

Located at Bishop's Landing on the Missouri River, the center exhibits replicas of boats used by Lewis and Clark in their famous expedition to the Pacific Ocean. The boats make an annual trek retracing portions of the journey.

Lewis and Clark Memorabilia *(top and bottom)*

The Boat House's upper level displays artifacts from the old Lewis and Clark Museum and diaramas by museum artist, Evangeline Groth, illustrating the Native American tribes Lewis and Clark encountered and the flora and fauna they catalogued. The Boat House is next door to Frontier Park where visitors can spread out a picnic or take a scenic walk or bike ride on Katy Trail, a route that runs parallel to the Missouri River and follows the first 225 miles of Lewis and Clark's expedition.

Historic St. Charles Train Depot

Built in 1892 by the Missouri, Kansas &
Texas Railway, the St. Charles Depot was the
easternmost stop on the line, carrying lumber,
fuel and grain to St. Charles and Weldon
Springs. It was moved to its present location
in Frontier Park in 1976.

Lewis and Clark Monument

Visible from the Katy Trail in Frontier Park, the fourteen-foot-high bronze monument honors the courageous explorers hired by President Thomas Jefferson to explore and chart a direct water route to the Pacific Ocean.

St. Louis Art Museum

Founded in 1879, the St. Louis Art Museum attracts thousands of visitors with an exceptional collection of art from virtually every culture and time period, the strongest of which is twentieth-century German art.

An Inspirational Setting

Designed by noted architect Cass Gilbert in the regal Beaux-Arts style, the St. Louis Art Museum is adorned with fountains that create a dramatic display of light and water. The world-class museum houses one of the most comprehensive fine art collections in America.

103

James S. McDonnell Planetarium (*above*)

One of the nation's leading space education facilities, the Planetarium at the St. Louis Science Museum features the unique Boeing Space Station with two levels of fascinating exhibits that show how astronauts eat, sleep, exercise and dress in space.

Flight Gallery (*opposite, top*)

On display at the Planetarium is a full-size replica of SpaceShipOne, the prize-winning design for the first commercial space flight. Also on exhibit are the provocative designs of all twenty-three contestants for the prestigious X Prize.

Dark Sky Show (*opposite, bottom*)

The Planetarium features much-anticipated thirty-minute "dark sky" shows in the StarBay, including *In Search of Distant Planets* and *Earth's Offshore Island—The Moon*. Afterwards the staff answers audience questions.

Scientist at Work *(top)*

Scientists are brewing up some interesting fun at the Science Museum. The Discovery Room is loaded with enjoyable hands-on exhibits and activities for young children to introduce them to the wonders of science.

Where Learning is a Blast *(bottom)*

Much like an educational arcade game, the hands-on activities at the Planetarium allow children to push buttons and turn handles and make things happen on other planets in our Solar System.

St. Louis Science Museum

One of St. Louis' famous, free museums, the Science Museum is a non-stop fun experience for all ages, with over six-hundred, hands-on exhibits on ecology, space and humanity, including exciting, life-size, animated dinosaurs.

City Museum of St. Louis *(top and bottom)*

Explore the unexpected! is the slogan of the City Museum of St. Louis. This huge warehouse of adventure features an enchanted forest, secret caves, passageways, a giant aquarium, a small circus, and a special museum of oddities. A school bus hanging off the build-ing's roof is a museum staple of startling interest. The size of two-and-a-half football fields, the museum provides activities and events for all ages.

Challenger Space Center *(top and bottom)*

Founded in 1986 by families of the astronauts tragically lost during the Challenger space shuttle mission, the Challenger Space Center is part of a growing school of forty-five centers located throughout the United States, Canada and the United Kingdom. Since opening in 2003, more than 9,000 visitors have been on simulated space missions, choosing either a voyage to Mars or a rendezvous with a comet.

Earl C. Lindburg Automotive Center

(top and bottom)

The Automotive Center at the Transportation
Museum has undergone major renovations.
Inside the ride is very cherry, with Model T's,
legendary racers, and Mustangs with thunder
down under—the original pony car.

Transportation Museum

Smithsonian Institution Curator Emeritus, John White, believes that St. Louis' Transportation Museum houses *"one of the largest and best collections of vehicles in the world."* Explore the sites of the first man-made railroad tunnels as well as over seventy locomotives. It's the most complete collection of national railway power assembled. Other attractions include streetcars, aircrafts and riverboat memorabilia.

Magic House *(above)*

The Magic House at the St. Louis Children's Museum features more than one-hundred, hands-on exhibits that make learning fun. Stimulating experiments like freezing your shadow on the wall or literally make your hair stand on end are sure to delight.

Lewis and Clark Adventure *(opposite)*

At the Magic House, patrons can learn the skills and ways of life of early explorers. Relive the expedition of Meriwether Lewis and William Clark and blaze a trail to the Pacific Ocean.

Worldways Children's Museum

For young children and adults, this museum makes faraway places suddenly seem close with interactive exhibits in realistic settings that help them experience the cultures and daily routines of people around the world. In the China exhibit, children sit in a red pagoda and learn to write the Chinese alphabet, make Chinese opera masks and other traditional gifts. They also visit a Chinese marketplace and learn how to use chopsticks.

Boat Picnic *(top)*

Next to a scenic mural of sister city Saint Louis in the West African country of Senegal, children sit around a colorful fishing boat or "pirogue" and learn about the traditional foods of this seacoast city thousands of miles away.

Climbing the Walls *(bottom)*

When children are climbing the walls at this delightful museum, it doesn't mean they are bored and fidgety; it just means they are having fun climbing a wall painted with fish and marine life.

115

Old Chain of Rocks Bridge *(above)*

Spanning one of the most scenic areas of the Mississippi River, the Old Chain of Rocks Bridge was constructed in 1929 as part of Route 66 and became known as an engineering marvel for overcoming the serious obstacles that the river presented.

Navigating the Towers *(opposite)*

The Chain of Rocks Bridge is famous for the twenty-two degree bend in its middle, which allowed southbound riverboats to avoid crashing into these two Gothic water intakes. Built in 1894, they serve as water intakes for the Chain of Rocks Water Treatment Facility.

**International Bowling Museum and
Hall of Fame** *(above and opposite)*

Bowling is one of the most popular sports today, with ninety-five million people playing around the world. This unique museum uncovers the cultural legacy of this 5000-year-old sport known as the "Sport of Kings."

Bowling was outlawed by King Edward III, promoted by King Henry VIII and has, ultimately, evolved into a popular professional sport as well as part of active every-day American life.

Shakespeare Festival (*above and opposite*)

Since 2001, the Shakespeare Festival of St. Louis has brought free, outdoor theater to audiences in centrally located Forest Park. In addition, the Festivals educational outreach program performs at some 96 schools annually.

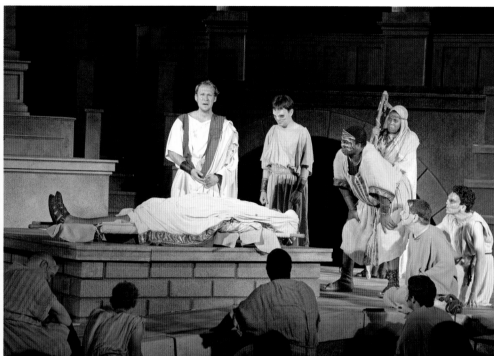

Sleepy Reptile

Children are fascinated by lizards in the
Hidden Forest, a jungle realm located at the
World Aquarium. This unique aquarium
offers a wide range of hands-on art and
animal attractions.

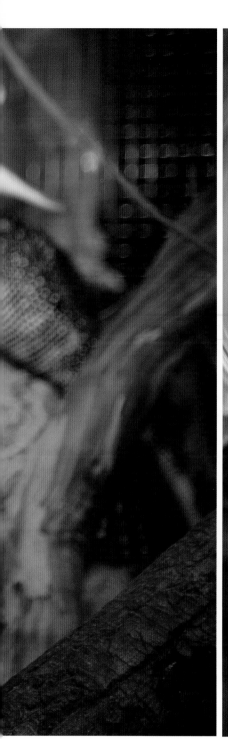

Fish Tunnel

Part of the City Museum, the World
Aquarium makes sure children experience sea
life from their perspective. Kids love crawling
through this clear tunnel that winds through
the water in the aquarium; it's almost like
swimming with the fish.

Fresh Produce at Soulard Farmer's Market

Locally owned businesses offer farm fresh fruits, vegetables and crafts year 'round at the Soulard Farmer's Market. Not only is it a common ground for shopping but people watching is fun too!

Soulard Farmer's Market

Soulard Market is the sole survivor out of
many open-air markets that have shared the
city's history. The farmer's market tradition
dates back to 1764 when St. Louis' far-think-
ing city planners set aside the land to use as a
farmer's market.

Pevely Farms Golf Club

Once a prosperous dairy show farm nestled in the picturesque Meramec River Valley, Pevely Farms has been reinvented as a "must play" championship 18-hole golf course by noted golf course designer, Arthur Hills.

Purina Farms *(top)*

An animal education center, Purina Farms conducts dog shows throughout the day that teach dog training tips and exhibit dog agility and skills. Cat lovers can visit the center's resident cats at a 28-foot-tall Victorian-style cat house.

Ted Drewes *(bottom)*

Ted Drewes has been selling his now-famous frozen custard to St. Louisans for decades. Repeatedly approached by offers to franchise, Drewes refuses, saying *"franchising could lead to mediocrity… and we just can't let that happen."*

Bill Grant

Award-winning photographer, Bill Grant, loves to travel and photograph the beauty around him, whether it is Hawaii, Mexico, Canada or his home state of Missouri. Even though he has lived here for twenty-three years, Grant continues to be amazed by the beauty and allure of Missouri. He spent six months photographing St. Louis for this book, always hoping to capture one, single, visual image that would personify St. Louis; but, he found it impossible. As a result, *St. Louis: A Photographic Portrait* celebrates a kaleidoscope of images that ultimately captures this great city. Grant shot most of these photographs with his Canon 5D digital camera. His photographs have been published in various magazines, calendars and brochures. Fine art prints are available on his website at www.visualjourney.com